WAR DAD

A Daughter's Story of How She Survived
the Damages of War on Her Father

Juju Sands

iUniverse, Inc.
New York   Bloomington

iUniverse books may be ordered through booksellers or by contacting:

iUniverse
1663 Liberty Drive
Bloomington, IN 47403
www.iuniverse.com
1-800-Authors (1-800-288-4677)

Because of the dynamic nature of the Internet, any Web addresses or
links contained in this book may have changed since publication and
may no longer be valid. The views expressed in this work are solely those
of the author and do not necessarily reflect the views of the publisher,
and the publisher hereby disclaims any responsibility for them.

ISBN: 978-1-4401-9042-1 (sc)
ISBN: 978-1-4401-9043-8 (ebook)

Printed in the United States of America

iUniverse rev. date: 1/12/2010

To my children, Michael and Jasmine,

whom I adore with all the life I have in me.

*Never stop achieving everything you
dream, but, in everything you do,*

keep your eyes on the Lord!

My Pledge to You

I was a lost girl with no direction and no future.

Then I gave birth to you.

The first time I held you, I knew

I wasn't going to let anything or anyone hurt you.

For you, it was going to be different.

I was in control now, and

I had the power to give you a good life.

So I sacrificed

and died to myself

and gave life

to the Christ within me.

A Heavenly Loan

Children are a gift from God.

They belong to Him, and we are only borrowing them.

We are responsible for giving them a

loving home, a mom, and a dad.

We are responsible for teaching them to

love God, love others, and love themselves.

And for showing them the way back to heaven.

Contents

Just for You

As I write this book, more than 100,000 American troops are currently in Iraq and Afghanistan, sacrificing to keep America safe. Out of the soldiers that have come home, an estimated three hundred thousand are living with post-traumatic stress disorder (PTSD). Over seven thousand suicides, either during combat or after the soldier comes home, have been reported. Nearly a third of our soldiers develop serious mental problems within three to four months after coming home. These figures are from cases that are tracked. Many soldiers live with PTSD silently and never get help. In 2008, the United States spent five thousand dollars per second on the Iraq war. Our government's veteran medical program is currently over one billion dollars short. These are astonishing figures! Yet, when our troops come home, the system often mistreats them, and they are forgotten. They desperately need quality long-term medical and psychological care, and the funding is not there. The current system our government has in place is not working.

Not only do the veterans suffer, but so do their families, especially their children. About one-third of children of deployed American soldiers are at high risk for developing psychological problems, mainly due to high levels of stress experienced by the at-home parent. It is known that the at-home parent must assume greater responsibility with taking care of all finances, keeping up the house, and maintaining the children and extended family. Many female partners and wives of veterans report experiencing more acts of family violence. This proves that there is secondary trauma to the family, spouses, and children, and I was one of them.

About seven years ago, I began to entertain the thought of writing a book about my experiences. I wanted to reach out to people on a large scale. When I prayed about it, I always felt a tug on my heart as if God was telling me I needed to, but it scared me. I am a natural talker. I have a good sense of humor and I love to make people laugh, but those qualities do not prepare a person to write an entire book. Having said that, let me warn you: I am not a professional writer. I write as the thoughts come to mind, as if I were sitting right next to you and speaking to you one-on-one. I want you to feel what I felt and what I'm feeling as I write. I have learned that physical pain, loss, hurt, and hopelessness have no education or social barriers. It doesn't matter what level of education you have or where you went to school. You will understand this book, and you will connect with all the feelings and emotions I have freely released straight from my heart. I have held nothing back.

If a person has a story to tell, regardless of the caliber of writing, the message will come through. My message: *There is hope!*

My goal is to reach out to women, young girls, and people from all types of lifestyles who have been affected by war. There are thousands of children, teenagers, young women, and young men that need to know they are not alone. The following pages are just a few stories about my childhood experiences. To write about it all would have taken too long. What you will read are fragments of memories, sometimes full accounts, of the traumatic situations I was exposed to at a young age because of my father's choices. For his choice to live a life of crime, for the heroin and drug abuse, for the alcohol abuse, for the anger, for the loss of a man, and for the loss of my dad, I blame the war in Vietnam.

At times, you might find it hard to believe that I'm still sane. In some parts of the book, I might seem angry or bitter. I guess I was, but I held it in. Better yet, I blocked those feelings out of my reality. It was the only way I was going to get through it. I only dealt with the feelings when I had to. Because I tried so hard to convince myself that I wasn't an extension of my dad and I was my own person, I can say today that I am not bitter. I know the Lord had mercy on me. He gave me the strength to survive, and He protected me through so many dangerous times. I can't tell you how thankful I am to Him. I have tried to dedicate my life to God hoping that, in doing so, I can show Him how grateful I am.

I keep one Bible verse very close to my heart, Matthew 6:33: "But seek first the kingdom of God and His righteousness, and all these things shall be added unto thee." It keeps me grounded. It keeps me focused and reminds me of my goal. We are to seek God first, live right, and He will take care of the rest. Matthew 6:33 says it all.

I believe each one of us is on a journey here on earth, and we are just passing through. What each one of us decides to do on our journey is entirely up to that person. God gives us free will. He doesn't force us to live our lives His way. We get to choose. I love reading true stories about people's lives because I learn so much about how they traveled their journey here on earth. I try to copy the things they did right and use them in my own life journey to help me succeed. We can all learn from each other. We might come from different backgrounds, upbringings, and cultures, but we are all the same inside.

When we truly know why we are here on this earth —our purpose— and we accept it, everything else takes a back seat. When I think about how many people need hope and help, my problems become so small. My purpose is to spread the hope that I found in a man who literally saved me from self-destruction. I am here to tell you that there is a way out through Christ! There is hope. I am here to warn you that our time is short; life is short, and one day Christ will come back for us, and we must be prepared. No one is promised a long life. I'm here to say that we should stop swimming in our own sorrow. We should get out there and help the poor, the needy, and kids who don't have parents or who need mentors. We should go anywhere where we can bring hope. God is looking down on us.

Throughout the book, I've included verses that remind me of God's promises. Write them down, and memorize them. They will become a part of your life. Make no mistake. You are not reading this book by accident; I truly believe that. I didn't write this book because I was bored. I wrote it specifically for you. I put my heart, tears, and sweat into this book. So as you read, grow.

Whoever loves instruction loves

knowledge,

but he who hates correction is

stupid.

A good man obtains

favor

from the Lord,

but a man of wicked intentions,

He will condemn.

Proverbs 12:1–2

For Those Who Find
It Hard to Believe

I love to watch *Oprah*. She is the big sister I never had. One day, as I took a short break from writing this book, I was able to catch a glimpse of a show. Some months ago, Oprah had interviewed an author who wrote a book about his experiences in his life, a rags-to-riches story. Shortly after that interview, it was exposed that the book was highly fabricated. I heard that people who bought the book wanted their money back because they thought they were reading a true story and they felt the author had lied to them. What I am telling you, and so much more, really did happen to me, and for the record, my story is just that: *my* story.

Some people who know me might disagree with the way I view my childhood. They have only seen me lead a normal life. I grew up, graduated from school, got a good job, got married, bought a house, and had two children. I live a very blessed life, so it might be difficult for some to believe I experienced the events I write about in this book. They might even disagree with the recollection of my facts. Well, to those people, I say, "Write your own book!"

When I was two years old, my parents were divorced. According to my mom, it was stipulated in the divorce papers that my dad was only allowed supervised visitation due to his violent nature. I spent one hour a week visiting, with my grandparents (his parents) as the supervisors. Before the divorce, I did not spend a lot of time with my dad. If anything, my mom and I spent more time trying to get away from him. He was extremely physically abusive to my mom, and he would physically and mortally threaten her and her family. I know I was only two years old when they divorced, but, when I think back that far, I do remember being afraid of him. I was little, but I knew when there was something wrong. It seemed as if a constant negative force lingered around me and my mom. So, because of that, I probably spent more time with my grandparents than with my dad before the divorce. I loved my grandparents so much, and I loved being with them. So, as I got older, I would beg my mom to let me visit them every weekend. She would succumb to my pleading and out went the hourly visitations each week. But unknown to my mom, the price I paid for trying to see my grandparents was hefty. You see, my dad would pick me up from my grandparents' house. My mom never knew how much time I spent with my dad after the divorce. My grandparents told me that if my mom ever found out, I would never see them again. So I suffered in silence. Every Sunday evening, my mom would pick me up. She would ask if I had a good visit. I would only tell her the positive parts of my weekend. The second I stepped into my mom's car, I also stepped into my second life, my good life. I wouldn't talk to anyone about the horror I had just experienced that weekend at my grandparents' house. Either way, no one ever asked. Who in their right mind would imagine the stuff I went through? I basically took on a different life, and I never mixed the two. Monday morning would come around. I'd wake up for school, shower in my beautiful bathroom, and put on my makeup in the separate vanity area. I'd get my little sisters ready for school and brush their hair. Then we'd go downstairs to eat breakfast. I'd turn on my state-of-the-art stereo system, listen to the morning radio show, and then run out for the bus. I loved seeing all my friends at school. They would get dropped off in their parents' fancy cars, and they had on the latest fashions. We lived in a very nice area, and I went to the best schools around. Thank you, Mom!

For the skeptics, I say this book is how I remember my life. The time frames were hard to pinpoint, but nevertheless, they happened. The book contains feelings and emotions I felt. It's my truth. No one else was there. He was my war dad, and this is my story.

This Is My Story, This Is My Song

All the days of my life I will praise you.

Because of you, now all is well,

and I am at rest.

You gave me peace, you gave me hope.

I will walk upright,

my eyes looking to the clouds, watching and waiting,

for I know

you will soon come back for me,

and I will be with you forever.

But for now, this is my story, this is my song.

Telling the Story for the First Time

The hardest thing to do is to put your emotions, your inner pain and hurt, and most of all your life out on the line.

This book has been on my heart for years. I have prayed so much about it. There have been times I thought about never telling anyone, but the Lord had different plans. I was too embarrassed and too ashamed. What would people think of me? But the Lord showed me that He was not going to let my dad's life, his sacrifices in Vietnam, go in vain. In my dad's death, the Lord was going to use me to tell our story and reach millions in all languages, all cultures, and all education levels. At times, I didn't want to think about writing this book because it seemed too big and too emotional. I would have to revisit the past and revisit the pain. But when I would least expect it, I would find myself in a situation that would remind me of writing my book. It haunted me!

One winter morning just before I decided to write this book, I was living in the Seattle area. It rained so much there that all I could do was clean my house, read, and eat. While cleaning up the house one morning, I had the television going in the kitchen. I went into another room to tidy up. From that room, I could hear a news piece about an army wife whose husband had just been deployed and how she was going to cope with being a single mom for a while. My heart broke for her. I thought about the emotional and mental condition in which her husband would return. He would never be the same. She should say good-bye to the man she knew. Shortly after that day, I was at the grocery store, buying our weekly groceries and minding my own business, when I turned into an aisle and I saw a young soldier dressed in full military attire. His head was shaved, and he had his military cap on. I stopped in my tracks and stared at him for what I thought was a quick second. I had to turn away because my eyes were full of tears, ready to drip down my face and ruin my makeup. But I wondered if he was afraid to go.

Was this his last trip to the store? Why did he enlist?

I couldn't help but think about when my dad was deployed. He was just as young as the soldier in front of me. I just knew I had to write about my story.

The following summer, we were living in Southern California again. Because we had not enjoyed a hot summer in Seattle, my husband and I decided to take the kids to the river for some family fun on the water. One hour into our trip, my kids got hungry, so we stopped for some famous hamburgers in Barstow, California. As I walked into the hamburger joint, a group of soldiers in army attire were standing around, waiting for their order. After I placed my order, I turned away from the cashier and looked around for a seat, but I was paralyzed. My body wanted to turn toward the group of soldiers, but I couldn't bear to look at them because I knew I would burst into tears, yet I had an extreme urge to go up to them, shake their hands, and thank them for their service. The first thing that came to mind was the book and the fact that I might be able to help one of their daughters, their sons, or their family members cope with what was to come. At the same time, I didn't want to because the idea of writing this book would get stronger and I didn't know if I could hold back the tears. But nevertheless, I went up to them, shook their hands, and thanked them. As I walked away, I felt so good. I just knew there was a connection. It felt right, and the desire to write this book became so much more powerful. I knew without a doubt, and with everything in me, that I had to speak up.

As I wrote certain chapters, there were times when I felt as if I had taken a knife and voluntarily sliced open every internal wound with my own hand. As I was writing the chapter about my grandparents, I had reached the point where I had to write about their death. It was so tough to write. As I recollected and typed each word, I could physically feel my heart breaking piece by piece. I began to sob as if they had just died. I put my face in my hands so my daughter, who was in the next room, wouldn't hear me crying, but she happened to walk into my office. I heard her at the door. As I looked up, I noticed she was startled. She began to slowly walk back out, but I called her back into my office and let her read the entire chapter I was writing. I never really told my kids what happened to me as a child. They just knew I had had a rough childhood.

I have seen hell on earth. Going through all the turmoil has made me strive to be better than what was expected for me. I refused to be a statistic! I know so many people who have always had everything they have ever wanted since childhood, and now they take life for granted. They live their lives making excuses for not achieving their goals.

They always blame someone else for their mistakes and misfortunes. As odd as it may sound, I feel a sense of gratitude for having experienced a rough upbringing and for having been a war daughter. At a young age, I experienced hurt, internal pain, loneliness, shame, and a sense of loss. These are feelings that many people do not experience until they have lived life a long time. Or maybe they never do—I don't know—but because of my experience, I sure did strive hard to rise up and be successful. War daughters and others affected by war can choose to turn the tables around and make better decisions. We can travel through life more cautiously, taking smarter steps. In doing so, we can hopefully make fewer mistakes.

I am very pleased with the direction in which my life has gone. I am proud of the situations and life decisions where I chose to do the right thing. Don't get me wrong. I was raised by a single mom from the hippy era, and I had a lot of freedom, so I wasn't perfect and I made a lot of irresponsible choices (Lord knows how many times He had to save me from my stupidity), but I always corrected my actions, asked for forgiveness, and got back on track to living for Christ.

As you read my story, you might get the feeling that I am angry and bitter and I have not put the past behind me. That is far from the truth. I am not angry at my dad, my mom, or myself. If anything, I thank my dad. He showed me that there really could be hell on earth. If I had not seen it with my own eyes, I might be naïve to this other world, to this behind-the-scenes life after war. It's funny how we never hear about this stuff on the news. Without my dad, I would have never written this book that is so filled with hope.

For those reasons and so many more, I write this book. My wish is that if you are a daughter of a war dad or a person who has suffered at the hands of one of your parents, you will gain strength and a sense of entitlement after reading this book. You will gain strength because you're not alone. Now you will know that it is possible to live a successful life. You will gain entitlement because children who are victims of a war dad or any other type of trauma have already experienced being in the pit of life. We deserve to live the best life we can. We need to believe that we are entitled to a good life, and we should strive to reach that goal.

I want to end this chapter with this: You will never forget what you went through or the pain you felt, but you must live each day unaffected. You cannot allow yourself to go there. Don't carry any baggage during your journey here on earth, especially someone else's! You must live each day as a winner! A survivor! Each day, you must march forward. And no matter what happens, don't *ever* look back!

Call upon

Me

in the day of trouble,

I

will deliver you,

and

you

will honor

Me.

Psalm 50:15

Reflecting Back in Time

I loved to visit them, but I hated it at the same time. To them, I was always an object of curiosity. They all wanted to touch me, caress my long, brown hair, and make comments about him. They would always reassure me that he was once a good man. They were my dad's family. Aunt Dee was always loud and happy, and she had a strong and hearty laugh. She was always laughing about something. Uncle Gary was more reserved, and he was a man of few words, but he loved to have a good time too. They had five children, my cousins, who were all older than I was. One of them, Gary Jr., would always have the latest records, and he would play them for me repeatedly on the record player.

God bless them! They would always try to make me feel welcomed and a part of the family, and I love them for that. But I always sensed that they secretly felt sorry for me. I could see it in their faces. Even as the family would sit around the kitchen table and talk about the good old times, I could sense their reservations about what they were saying. There was always a silence after each story.

Were they trying to shield my little heart from the pain?

They knew about the drugs, jail sentences, and abuse my dad was inflicting on my grandparents, but I know they were not aware of the severity of it. They didn't know how bad he really was. As the family would remember the good old days, I wanted to scream out loud and tell everyone to shut up!

I wanted them to know that the man they were talking about wasn't the man I knew. The man the family was talking about, their man, was fun, generous, gentle, funny, loving, caring, and an all-around good guy. The man I knew was violent, angry, volatile, psychotic, a drug addict, a woman beater, a womanizer, a criminal, and a danger to me, himself, and, most of all, society.

It was the early 1960s. They were living in a nice upper middle-class area. When my dad was in high school, my grandparents decided to move. They bought property in a lower middle-class, blue-collar area. There were families with a lot of children, parents, uncles, and aunties. My grandpa purchased a large piece of land with three houses on the lot. The property sat at the top of the hill of a busy main street. It had a two-level duplex apartment building and a large one-story home that needed a lot of work before my grandparents could live in it. East Los Angeles has such good memories for me, like memories of my grandma's cooking, gardening with my grandma, and climbing the guava tree and sitting on a branch and eating guavas until I was sick to my stomach. Then I'd go up again the next day and do it all over again.

And yet, if I allow myself, I can also remember a lot of the bad memories and the hell I experienced there. I can best describe my feeling about these bad memories by thinking of the scene at the end of the movie *Carrie*, where Carrie's friend goes to visit her grave. There was an eerie silence in the movie theater; spooky music was playing in the background. As the friend bends down to put flowers on the grave, suddenly, Carrie's hand pops up from the dirt of the grave and grabs the friend's hand! Do you remember that jolt and sudden shock of seeing the hand grab her and how it scared you? That is the best description I can give you as to how I feel when I think about those memories.

Back to my grandparents' house. They lived in the top-level apartment. The one below was a rental. The large house on the side of the apartments was used for storage. They had planned to eventually fix up the big house and live in it, but it never happened. The inside of my grandparents' apartment was turquoise blue, and hanging over the windows were light beige curtains with big brown flowers that hung in the one room that was used as the living room, the main bedroom, and the dining room. It had one bathroom, one bedroom, and a very small kitchen. Outside was a semi-sturdy, white wooden flight of stairs that led to the entrance room of the apartment. In that entrance room was the refrigerator, a freestanding fruit holder, and a parrot named Perico. Perico always announced when a visitor was coming up the stairs. It was an extremely small house, and it wasn't in the best condition, but to me, it was a home, my grandparents' home. To me, it was the best home in the world.

The yard was huge. The houses sat at the back end of the property, so there was a lot of room for fruit trees (they had every kind of fruit tree you could think of) and bushes of white, pink, red, yellow, and multicolored roses. There were medicinal herbs, herbs for cooking, and just about every plant species you could think of. My grandmother watered the entire yard for hours every day by hand with a water hose. She tended to her garden just as well as she tended to her family. But behind the doors of that house was a secret that would be held for years until my grandmother's death.

Early in their marriage, my grandparents lost hope of ever having children. My grandmother was pregnant four times. She miscarried twice. The other two children died very early in life. During a trip to Texas to visit family, my grandparents stopped to visit an aunt. While visiting, she told my grandparents that her daughter had just had another baby and she couldn't afford him. The baby was lying in a playpen, and he was sick. They did not know what was wrong with him, but he was slowly falling into extreme conditions. My grandmother walked up to the playpen, and there he was, lying silently. He had a high fever, and it was evident that he needed medical attention. My grandmother immediately felt sorry for him, and she offered to take him back to California with her. After hours of visiting and a lot of talking, the baby's mom decided to give him to my grandparents to raise him as their own. That day, the entire family was sworn to secrecy. No one was allowed to tell my dad that he was really someone else's son.

Before they arrived back to California, his birth certificate was changed, and little Robert officially belonged to my grandparents. In my grandparents' mind, this little boy who was brought out of poverty was going to have the best life ever. My grandparents had money, and my dad got everything and anything he wanted. They once bought him a 1956 Corvette. He was the talk of the neighborhood. He was tall, dark, handsome, and rich, and he drove a nice car. He was very spoiled, and he experienced envy from other kids in the neighborhood.

School came easy to my dad. Although he wasn't the top student, he really didn't struggle in the basic education system. At a young age he was very involved with music. He played the clarinet so well that he joined a local jazz band of young musicians. I have one picture of the group. My dad is holding his clarinet, and he is dressed in a somewhat military-like band uniform. In the picture, he is smiling and you can see his little teeth. When I see that picture, it reminds me of how my teeth looked when I was little. I have to hold on to those little things. It might seem so meaningless, but it helps me to connect with my dad in a good way. His smile as a child is the same one I had.

But you, woman of God,

flee from all this

and pursue righteousness

Godliness,

faith,

love,

endurance,

and

gentleness.

1 Timothy 6:11

War Daughters

During the Vietnam War, young boys, starting at the age of seventeen years old, were being called into the military, whether they wanted to fight or not. They had no choice in the matter. Los Angeles seemed to have many boys who were drafted. I can't begin to tell you how many girls I grew up with whose fathers were Vietnam vets. It always seemed like those girls were the ones with all the problems. Either they had personal issues or there were problems in the family. It seemed as if this group (of which I was a part) was always looking to fit in. It wasn't that we were misfits or unwanted. It's just that either our home situation was not like the other lucky girls or we ourselves were having issues. Although I was surrounded by girls just like me, looking back, I didn't feel like I could tell anyone about anything I was going through. I didn't have a confidant.

I was too embarrassed to let people know my situation. I thought if they knew the truth about my dad or if they knew that I was being raised by a single mom, they would not want to hang out with me or they might look at me differently. Of course, the people in my townhouse complex and my closest friends knew about the situation with my mom, but they definitely did not know about my dad. I would never talk about him.

I was not yet born when my dad went to war, but that didn't exclude me from the repercussions of it. Many girls out there will never even know their dads because they were killed in the war. I sometimes wished my dad would have died in Vietnam. I know that is such a bad thing to say, but I really did feel that. My father was a casualty of the war, even though he returned. The life we would have had was gone. There were many of these other casualties out there. Some girls did have their dads come back from the war, only to have their parents separate or divorce because of the stress brought on by the negative change in the man. Some girls had their dads make it back from the war, only to find them very angry, distant, antisocial, and suffering from PTSD. Those little girls grew up in a very angry and abusive environment. They witnessed divorce and became a statistic. They witnessed physical abuse and found themselves in the same situation as adults. They witnessed drug addiction and sometimes fell into it themselves. The effects of war can live on from generation to generation if someone does not halt the effects. Someone has to be strong enough to bring about a change.

Regardless of the circumstances, how are young girls living in any of these situations supposed to grow up to be strong, confident women? How are we supposed to raise our own children and instill high morals and standards? How are we to know how to have healthy marriages if we weren't taught how to respect, love, honor, cherish, and trust our husbands?

In a world with no war, parents would have loved each other and stayed married. They would have taken us to church every Sunday. We would have enjoyed Sunday dinners as a family. In an ideal world, Dad would have never called Mom any names. Dad would have never cheated on Mom. Mom and Dad would have loved each other through thick and thin and worked on their marriage. "Daddy's little girl" would have been a true and sacred title. In a normal world, a girl would grow up strong and confident and have high self-esteem, nurtured by her parents. In a normal world, a girl wouldn't have to teach herself these things. In a normal world, would there ever be a war daughter?

Don't let anyone look down on you

because you are young,

but set an example

for the believers

in speech, in life, in love, in faith,

and in purity.

1 Timothy 6:11

War Moms

My mom had been an extremely beautiful girl. She had a light complexion, beautiful skin, gorgeous, light brown hair, and a face that screamed innocence and naïveté. She grew up during the days when the man of the house was the boss. She had that "Beaver Cleaver" way of thinking. She came from very humble beginnings, but that didn't matter to her because, in general, life was good. She was the apple of her daddy's eye. She loved her father so much. She looked up to him, and he could do no wrong. She knew her daddy was going to get them to a better place. Even if they had to stay living in that neighborhood, she knew she was safe. He was her hero.

My grandmother had seven children, and my mom was the fourth in line. She was the daughter who always thought she was better than the average girl. She was a goody-two-shoes who was going to do everything in her power to be different. She knew she was better than the drugs, the gangs, and the trouble that was around her. She helped my grandmother a lot with the younger children. To this day, she is still very protective of her brothers. She loves them more than they know.

One day, her daddy was taken to the hospital because of a bad fall. He had broken his ankle and his leg. He was six foot two and two hundred and thirty pounds. While in the hospital, he developed double pneumonia and became very ill. The doctors decided to keep him in the hospital a few weeks or until the pneumonia cleared. One afternoon, my mother accompanied my grandmother to the hospital. In those days, children were not allowed to enter the patient's room, but my mom wanted so badly to see her dad. So she pretended she had to use the restroom. As she ran down the hall toward the restrooms, she stopped at his room and stuck her head into the doorway. He looked toward the door and saw his little girl standing there.

As their eyes met, she told him, "I love you, Daddy."

He responded, "I love you too."

If she had only known that would be the last time she would ever hear her daddy's voice or look into his eyes.

The next morning, my mom got on the city bus and was on her way to school when she noticed my grandmother running down the street toward the hospital. All day in school, she had an awful feeling. When she got home from school that afternoon, everyone was there: aunts, uncles, and grandparents.

My mom asked, "What's going on?"

They told her, "Your dad died."

He had had a massive heart attack, and the doctors couldn't save him.

Because my grandmother had seven kids and was now a widow, the family thought it would be best if the kids would each go to live with a different relative. My grandmother was devastated at the thought and refused. She told the family she was keeping her seven children, no matter what.

Their lives changed forever. Now nothing was easy.

My grandmother sold their home and spent all the profits from the sale unwisely. Before my grandfather's death, my grandmother had been the best mother she could be; she tended to the family with love. After my grandfather's death, she began to drink a lot and became a full-fledged alcoholic. With my grandmother basically checking out, things were scarce. Many times, there was no food in the house, and the younger children didn't have proper school attire. No longer was my mom's dad there to provide and care for the family, and my mom felt helpless. Her grades in school were suffering. This whole change was too much for her to handle, so she decided to drop out of school and try to make things better at home. She got a job and worked hard to provide for her little brothers and the home. But she was lost. She had no direction.

My mom has never gotten over the death of her daddy. Even at sixty years old, she still cries as she tells me about him. An incredible emotional bond is alive within every little girl who knows her dad. Whether a girl loses her dad to war, sickness, or any form of death, she loses a part of herself. She goes through life searching for that love.

My parents met when my mom was in junior high school and my dad was in high school. My mom lived down the hill from my dad. She lived two houses down from where my grandmother and I would stop and take a break from carrying the groceries up the hill. They eventually began to date. In the years to come, my dad would take my mom everywhere and anywhere her heart desired. He would take her and her two little brothers to the mountains, the drive-in theatre, and hamburger shops. My dad would buy my mom nice gifts and spoil her. When he knew my mom didn't have food at home, he would give her money to buy food for the family. He was pretty good to her. It was very easy for my mom to fall in love with my dad. He filled that gap, and my mom clung to that as long as she could, even after the war changed him. When they divorced, she continued her search for that love in other relationships.

Back in those days, society was not accustomed to the idea of single moms. That became more prevalent in the late 1960s when divorce was rising. At that time, there was also a huge stigma on divorced women. They were viewed as failures. My mother went through two unsuccessful marriages, and she found herself alone with three girls to raise. She never really had a good grip on life and how to live it successfully. Don't get me wrong. She was also very strong. I know it sounds contradictory, but she did overcome so much, from losing her dad at a young age, to her mother's alcoholism, to beatings from my dad, to being a single mom. For that, I must give her credit.

It is now possible for women to show their strength and have power and status. We make more money. We're running companies, homes, and families and still keeping sane. The majority of women I speak to feel they do not need a man to complete them. The single moms of today, in my opinion, seem to know how to cope with life and childrearing better than the single moms of the 1960s. My mother was overwhelmed with trying to raise three girls on her own, work, pay rent, put food on the table, and still keep her sanity.

My mother's strength taught me that I could overcome any situation in life. Growing up, my mom always laughed at her personal problems. She always minimized a stressful situation. I didn't see frailty in her. She was always so strong.

During one emergency situation, we packed our bags and left our home for good. We were literally homeless. We had no place to sleep that night. We could have gone to my grandma's house, but my mom refused to humiliate herself in that manner, so we ended up at a motel. It sure wasn't my nice bedroom in my beautiful, two-story townhouse, but my mom assured us it was only for one night. She set up the situation to be an adventure. I led my mom to believe that we were fine, but my sisters and I were very scared. We knew there was a possibility that our lives as we knew them were over, but my mom never shed a tear. That's just the way she was. Being strong in any situation is something for which she is still known.

My mom made many choices that at the time she thought were good, but she was so oblivious to what was going on in my life. I don't think she knew that kids watch and copy their parents. She didn't realize I was watching her every move and being affected emotionally by her choices. I think she didn't want to know. She couldn't handle it. She had to believe that everything was under control or she might have lost it. She might have had a nervous breakdown like a lot of my friends' mothers did.

As we got older, my sisters and I sure did throw a lot of stuff in her face. At times, my sisters and I blamed her for anything that went wrong in our lives. We would associate our shortcomings to the way she raised us. I feel badly about doing that to her. I know now and understand that she was—and still is—fragile, deep inside. I used to think that maybe I would have not made many of the bad choices I made in my life if my mom would have known how to handle the emotional side of being a single mother. But who am I fooling? I have to stop blaming my mother for my choices in life. If you are blaming your mom, you need to stop and take responsibility for your own actions.

Our moms are human. There's no manual on how to raise kids. In most situations, there is no mentor guiding our mothers through the tough childrearing years. Most of the time, they have no one to turn to. In my situation, the man of the home went to war and came back on drugs. When he returned, he was angry and abusive. He didn't know how to be a father, a husband, or the leader of the home. So now you not only have a war mom, but also a war daughter. One man going to war affects both women.

I have the utmost respect for war moms. They have to go it alone. They have to stay at home, wait for their men, fight stressful emotions, and still try to raise their children to be well-rounded human beings. There is no one to hold them at night and tell them that everything is going to be all right. Often, even after the war dad, the soldier, returns home, their problems don't end. They begin.

Now I think I understand why my mom always felt she had to find a father figure for us. She was trying to get it right just once and give us the family life she so desired for herself as a child.

Be careful to obey all

these regulations I am giving you

so that it may always go well with you

and your children after you

because you will be doing

what is good and right in the eyes of the

Lord your God.

Deuteronomy 26:2

Did He Have Any Good in Him?

My father was so talented in music. He played many instruments. The clarinet was the first instrument he learned. I truly believe music was his calling. I was about nine years old the first time I heard him play the clarinet. I went to visit my grandparents for the weekend, and I hoped my dad wouldn't show up. Early in my visit that weekend, my heart hit the floor.

In order to enter my grandparents' property, you had to get through these very heavy, metal swinging gates. My grandfather would put a heavy chain around the handles of the gates and insert a padlock to secure the property at night. During the day, you could get into the property by lifting the chain out of one gate and pushing it open. In doing so, the chain would jingle so loudly that we could hear it all the way to the back of the property and into the house.

I heard the gate opening. I looked out the window and saw him walking down the driveway. Every single time I would see him walking down the driveway, my stomach would turn. I swear I wanted to throw up! I knew he was coming to take me. But that day was different. He was at peace. He was so calm. He came in and sat on the dining table and watched TV with me. I don't remember what triggered the talk about music, but he went into the bedroom and brought out a little black box with a thin rope tied around it holding the case closed. He untied the rope and opened the case. Inside was the clarinet he played as a young boy. I can still remember the smell of that case. He assembled the clarinet as if he had never left it. He wet his lips and propped the mouthpiece perfectly on his bottom lip. As he blew into the instrument, I couldn't believe he was creating that angelic sound, that beautiful music. He became another person in my eyes. Other than making me, I don't think he had ever created something so beautiful. He played an old song from the 1960s.

In between the notes, he sang the words to the song. He had such a classy and distinguished voice, so gentle and mellow, like Smokey Robinson.

I was enjoying my daddy so much, but I began to notice his head would slowly droop. He would doze off between measures. I tried to tell myself that he was just sleepy. I wanted that moment to be wholesome and innocent. For those few minutes, he seemed normal, just like a real person on my level and in my world. For those few minutes, it felt as if all the shady people in his life, all the problems, all the drugs, and all the ugliness disappeared. It was the one time he was into me.

I wanted so badly for the dozing off to be pure exhaustion. But a side effect of heroin is a constant dozing off or falling asleep instantly. There is no way he felt the special moment we had just shared. It was all me, and I had to be okay with that. To this day, I cannot speak to anyone who is intoxicated. When someone has been drinking and is beyond tipsy, I shut down. Their mind is not present, and I no longer want contact with that person until he or she is sober.

There was one other time I felt proud of my dad and his music. I had not seen him in about a year because he had been locked up in a state penitentiary for drugs or attempted murder; who knows what the charges were. I called my grandparents to let them know I would be visiting that weekend. They told me they had heard from my dad. They said he had been released and he was doing well. He was leading the band at a little church in Valinda, California, and he wanted us to go see him.

That Sunday, we found someone to take us to the church, because my grandpa could no longer drive. As the band began to play, I was dumbfounded! The band sounded really good. The band members were all in sync, and my dad had every instrument playing on key. He was singing and praising the Lord! The little church was filled with people singing, clapping, and enjoying the music. I could not believe that my dad, the mess-up, had the whole church rocking! I was beyond happy. I was so proud of him. I thought for sure that he was cured. I also felt a sense of guilt come over me because I had doubted God's power.

Did he really turn his back on his first love, heroin? Was he really done with the life of crime he was so entangled in? Maybe he was a changed man this time.

Soon thereafter, I learned about the California penal system. When a convict wants to stay out of jail or be paroled, he makes a plea to the judge to enter into a recovery home in place of being incarcerated. It so happened that my dad chose a religious men's home in which to detox.

It seems like he did that often, but I was too young to understand. I guess this church offered that program.

After that Sunday, a few months passed. I still had no contact with my dad, but it didn't matter because he was doing well and things were going to be different. He was getting better—until one weekend visit to my grandparents' home. When I arrived that Saturday morning, my grandpa told me that my dad was now living in an apartment down the street, which was within walking distance. I was so happy! He actually had his own place.

It was a sunny day, and I had just enjoyed my favorite breakfast, which my grandma would cook every Saturday morning: two eggs over easy, potatoes steamed in tomato sauce, a hot dog split in half and pan-fried in Rex lard, and flour tortillas. After breakfast, I decided to take a walk over to my dad's new place. The apartment was located on the second level. As I walked up the stairs, I heard people talking, and the television was loud. I knew he wasn't alone. I was a very shy little girl, and I didn't want to meet new people, but I really wanted to see my dad. As I entered the apartment, I saw a sister from the church.

He said, "You remember Elaine. She's from the church."

I asked, "Are you both living in the apartment?"

He said, "She let me move in. She's a very good woman; she's good people."

I was young and shy but not stupid. I knew they were living together, and I was so hurt. My disappointment turned into anger really quickly. I was so mad at my dad.

What a hypocrite!

As for Sister Elaine, I felt sorry for her because I knew she was going to pay a hefty price. She had no idea who she had let into her home.

Elaine had cooked a late breakfast, and they were just about to eat. I was trying to keep my composure and remain polite, so I sat down on the couch and pretended to watch television. I couldn't look at him, much less at Elaine. I was completely disgusted. My dad sat at the dining table, and she served him his food. When she put the plate down in front of him, steam was coming from the hot food, but it wasn't appealing to me. The anger had overpowered me.

My dad told Elaine, "Serve Juju a plate."

I said, "I'm not hungry."

So she didn't serve me. He got so mad because he took that as Elaine treating me badly. In his twisted mind, she should have obeyed him. His voice began to escalate. He got up from the table, left his food, and went into the hallway. He then called for her to go into the bedroom. I could hear them arguing. Then I could hear her crying and screaming. I knew what was happening. She was getting beaten by the animal with whom she was sinning. I quietly walked out of the apartment and put the whole situation behind me.

No, I didn't call the police. No, I didn't help her. I couldn't! I was scared, fragile, young, and mad. All I kept telling myself is that she knew better.

My young central nervous system couldn't handle another violent situation. From what I have learned, some people block out traumatic experiences in life as a form of survival. That is just what I did. Shortly after that incident, he relapsed. I was so disappointed and humiliated.

What was the family going to say? What would the neighbors say? What were the church members going to think?

The chance to redeem our name, my name, and my face was once again gone. I was embarrassed to be his daughter. I wanted to hide myself from the world. I thought he knew the power God could have on a life. I thought he would trust God to change him. I actually had hope.

My dad ended up in jail again, and I don't know for what, maybe domestic violence. During his stay, he met a woman, Larie. She was a friend of a friend, and she began to visit him while he was locked up. Larie had a little girl named Cathy. Larie was very good to my dad. When he got out, they were married. Larie was tall and dark, and she wasn't easy on the eyes. She had a severe facial skin condition that caused small wart-like bumps on her face. But she was always good to me, and she never treated me badly. She had a good heart, but she made very bad choices in men.

After they married, my dad and Larie moved to a small, green, one-bedroom trailer in El Monte, California. The trailer park was on asphalt, which had cracks all over and no grass anywhere. It was very dirty and rundown, the raunchiest place I had ever seen back then. Living at the trailer park was probably the most stability my dad had in years. I had never had the opportunity to see him live a regular life and do everyday chores before.

One day, my dad got in a high-strung mood to clean the trailer for a pregnant Larie. (The baby later died in her womb.) But he took it overboard. Everything had to be sparkling clean. I don't know if he got that from the military, if he was coming down from a heroin fix, or if he really was a clean person. The trailer was so small that you could not pass in the hallway without bumping into the other person, so there wasn't much to clean.

As he was finishing up, he told us, "Sit on the couch. I'm going to mop the floor."

I knew he wasn't mentally stable when I saw him searching for floor-cleaning products. He knew good and well there weren't any in the trailer. He searched all over as if the cleaning products would suddenly appear.

Here we go again.

Suddenly, he went into the bathroom and took the only bottle of cologne he had, Oleg Cassini. He began to splash it all over the floor. With a wet rag, he wiped down the little piece of linoleum that was the entire trailer floor until it was clean and smelled fresh. I had never seen anything like that before. My mother never mopped with cologne or perfume. I knew he wasn't right, but what could I do? I had no choice but to store that in my memory as my dad trying to be good to his wife.

One day, I was with my dad, Larie, and Cathy. We were in Los Angeles, and we were trying to get back to his trailer in El Monte, and we were walking the streets. We kept walking for hours. I don't know what he was thinking. He had picked me up from my grandparents' home, and he was taking me to his trailer for the weekend. The only problem was that the trailer was about twelve miles away and he did not own a car. We often walked or took the city bus to wherever he was taking me. If we were walking, he would tell me to put my thumb out. This meant to hitchhike. I know he was from the hippy era when hitching a ride was viewed as somewhat normal, but it wasn't for me. I hated it. I was so humiliated, and I felt so low. I would sometimes put on a sad face to try to coerce people into giving us a ride. I was afraid of him, so I didn't argue. I just did it. I was a ten-year-old hitchhiker.

That day, we got as close as I could get us by hitchhiking, but we were still very far. I wasn't having any luck that day. No one wanted to give a family of four a ride. So he told us we would be walking a long time. He was so mad. I knew it was only a matter of time before he blew up.

What would it be this time? Was he going to beat Larie again in front of Cathy?

As we were walking, he looked at Cathy's and my shoes.

He told Larie, "They need new shoes."

He has money to get me shoes!

I was so pleased at his gesture. So we came across this little shop that sold a bit of everything. Against the wall, way in the back of the store, was a huge section of flip-flops.

My dad said, "Go try some on, and pick the ones you want."

Wow! My dad is buying me a pair of shoes. He must be doing well!

So Cathy and I happily chose our colors and quickly put them on. We walked around the store to test them out.

He then looked at Larie and told her to take us and leave the store. *Oh God!*

I had a horrible feeling in the pit of my stomach. He was going to make us steal the shoes. I wanted to throw up and scream out for help! I wanted someone to save me from this monster, and I was so mad at myself for actually putting my heart in a vulnerable state and believing he was actually buying me shoes. What a fool I was! I felt so sorry for the little Asian guy behind the counter. I didn't know if he was going to be beaten or stabbed or if he would even survive. Sure enough, my dad began to tell the guy that we needed new shoes. He told him we had to walk far and we didn't have money to buy the shoes. That didn't go well with the little Asian guy. They began screaming at each other, and I could see my dad's temper escalating.

The Asian guy finally said, "Get out! Take the shoes and leave!"

That was the first and the last pair of shoes my dad ever "bought" for me. I can't help but feel sorry for him. As I write this, my heart is so heavy. In his sick, drug-infested mind, his kids needed shoes and he was going to get them for us. I know it's sick, but I have to remember that everyone tells me he had been a very giving person.

Was this event a part of that giving side of him?

It's weird to say, but I can laugh at this now. I think of some of the things he did and I know he just wasn't right. He didn't have his right mind. He did things that you and I would never think of doing and even try to justify them. A little girl never forgets things like that. The feelings can stay so fresh in your memory. I guess you never get over it. You just have to put it behind you. It's in the past, and my life is different now. I want to believe he had a soft spot for mankind, for life. I want to believe in what so many people have told me about my dad in his pre-war days. But after reading this, what do you think?

He who trusts in his riches,

will fall,

but

the righteous will flourish

like foliage.

Proverbs 11:28

When Did It Happen?

Was it the first toke? Was it the first beer? Was it the first party? When and where did the transformation happen from having a good time to when the first needle went into his arm? Was it in Vietnam? Did he have these inclinations before he left? Not from what I am told. Or could it be that the pain of a soldier is so severe and so brutal that it takes them to a world of self-destruction? Where was that voice we all have that tells you "Don't do it!" And why can't some people stop?

The war, the drugs, and the heroin took my daddy away. I felt as if I were so small and meaningless in his life in comparison to the drugs. I was tired of him taking me with him to get his fix. I didn't want to see him get arrested anymore. I didn't want to feel humiliation anymore. Each time he was in jail, he would detox and be in a normal state of mind. Then I would plead with him to stop his lifestyle. Each time, he would promise he would change when he got out. But it never happened. He sold himself to heroin. The moment the needle went into his arm for the first time, he might as well have put me up for adoption. As I sit here and write, I get a tingle in my arm. To this day, I cannot watch a needle go into anyone's arm. Although I am strong now through my faith in God, I can still be so weak to the memories, the memories of him. The painful feelings can return instantly. If I hear a song that reminds me of him, I get an awful, sinking feeling in my stomach. I can't allow myself to stay there though. To do so would only set me back, so I can't allow anything to steal the inner happiness I now have.

When I was around nine or ten, I knew my dad was on drugs, but I didn't know what that really meant. I knew he drank a lot. He would always have a can of beer or a bottle of Thunderbird wine concealed in a brown bag. When he had extra money, he would splurge on a bottle of gin. I always knew when he had been drinking gin because he had a strong, weird scent to him and he would get very vulgar, angry, scary, and mean. When he was in this frame of mind, I was the only person who could calm him. I didn't know that when he didn't have money for his next fix, he would try to patch the withdrawal pain with hard liquor. The liquor was no match to the high he would get from heroin. If he didn't get a fix, he would become extremely angry, and beat, curse, and rip-up the house, and then take off. All hell would break loose, literally. He would commit a robbery or beat up one of his girlfriends and take her money. Or he'd abuse my grandpa until my grandpa would give him some money. Nevertheless, the cops were always called. If we were lucky, they would take him away to jail. He always abused my grandparents, verbally and physically, for money to buy heroin. But my grandparents were living off of Social Security and the little rent money they collected. So I began to learn that the outbursts were because he needed the next fix to prevent him from getting physically sick. I didn't know how widespread this addiction was until one night at the trailer.

It was dark out, and I was watching TV with Cathy. My dad told us, "Go outside."

Outside!

It was dangerous to be outside at night, especially in that raunchy trailer park. I didn't know what was happening, but I did as I was told. Although my dad never laid a hand on me and I didn't feel he would ever hurt me, I never wanted to find out. So I did as I was told. Little by little, shady, lowlife people began to arrive at the trailer. I was playing tag with Cathy to kill time. I saw this couple walking toward us. The lady was so drunk that she could hardly stand. I had never seen a person in that state, so intoxicated and so incoherent.

They walked up to me. "Do you know where Robert lives?"

I looked at the lady in amazement or maybe concern. She literally scared me. Her eyes were rolling back as she tried to speak. Her words were slurred, and her hands were all over the place. My heart fell to my stomach. I could not believe that my dad was going to let them in our house. I walked them over to the trailer and knocked on the door. My dad opened the door and I told him, "These people are looking for you."

By that time, the little trailer was packed with people, people I had never seen in my life. My dad looked at me with such a different look in his eyes.

With an angry, deep voice, he said, "Stay outside."

I couldn't believe he had spoken to me with that tone, so I decided I was going to find out what they were doing in there. I searched around for something I could stand on so I could peek into the window. I found some bricks, and I piled them up. I stood on top of them and tiptoed to raise myself up to the window level. Through a small gap in the curtain, I was able to see one of the men in there. Then I saw something I wish I could prevent any child from ever seeing. I saw the rubber band go around his arm and the needle go in.

Then I heard someone say, "The kids are looking in."

I got down as fast as I could and hid under the window. I stayed in a squat position for a few minutes, planning my escape, but it seemed to get quieter and quieter in the trailer until there was complete silence. Although I had been exposed to so much, I had never witnessed the actual act of drug use and I didn't know how fast the drugs took effect. So I didn't understand why they were all so quiet. That night, I figured out that heroin takes immediate effect. Except for Larie, they were all high. (She didn't use drugs until later in their relationship.) I quietly put the bricks back and went off to play. One by one, I saw them leave the trailer.

Something changed that night. There was no longer any hope. It was real. It was etched in stone. No one could tell me differently. My father was a junkie who was addicted to heroin. I knew I was in over my head.

How could I compete against his new child named heroin?

He was no longer my daddy. I had lost him forever. He became one of those people, a lowlife. Any speck of respect I had held for him as my father was gone. I felt superior to him. I felt he wasn't mentally on a normal level, like me. There was no talking to him anymore. I can't explain the thoughts and feelings that were going through my mind. He had once again disappointed and hurt me, and I would never let my guard down with him again. My heart was hardened even more so that night. The sick father-daughter relationship I had so hung onto was over. I still wonder about the first time he stuck a needle into his arm.

Where was he? Who was he with? Where was I? Why couldn't he stop?

Whenever I recall these events, I feel so gross and so dirty. I can't believe I was actually in that environment at one point in my life.

I am convinced that the Lord has shielded my heart from total destruction. To be able to live the life I am now living, He must have intervened. There is no other explanation. I may not know all things about life, and there are many places I have not yet been and opportunities I did not have, but, regardless, I am sure of one thing: God is real! I can feel Him in my soul. Every day, when I look into the eyes of my children, open the front door to my beautiful home, pet my dogs, and open my refrigerator and see the abundance of food in it, I see the evidence of the mercy He has on me. And that same God is there for you too. Get on your knees and pray day and night until you hear from Him. Pray day and night for His mercy and grace in your life. Pray day and night. It's the only way.

Pray

Praying on my knees is where I find you.

It's where I surrender.

It's where you talk to me.

It's where I find wisdom.

It's where I find peace.

It's where you will make me the woman you desire me to be.

Humiliation to Last a Lifetime

It was raining and cold outside, so my grandmother made me put on a heavy coat before we left the house. As I approached the guard at check-in inspection, he asked another guard about what to do with me because I was a little girl. It wasn't the first time I had gone to see my dad in jail; we frequented the Los Angeles County Men's Central Jail. But it was the first time I had stepped into a state prison, the California State Institution for Men in Chino, California. The guards began to talk amongst themselves. There was a lot of commotion and voices getting louder. I didn't understand what the fuss was over me, but I wanted to cry. I wanted to run out of there, but the line was going out the door, and I was trapped.

Aunt Dee pleaded, "Let her in."

One of the guards yelled, "She'll have to be searched."

The inspection guard looked down at me. He quickly and gently patted down my front, from my shoulders to my knees. He then spun me around, patted my back area, and let me through. I was so scared! Oh the humiliation of having a strange man pat you down simply to see your daddy. Thank God, Grandma had made me put on a heavy coat that morning. It was the only thing that shielded me from feeling fully violated.

Having to go through that put me (mentally and emotionally) in a different class. I was now somewhat associated with those people who had ties to criminals. You have no idea what that does to a little girl. I did not want anyone to know, not even family, but everyone already did. The whole neighborhood knew who I was. I was Robert's daughter. The moms in the neighborhood didn't want their kids to play with me; I wouldn't have let my kids play with me either.

On Mondays, when I would go back to my normal life at school, I never said anything about my weekend. My mom didn't know what type of weekend I had had. She simply thought that I had had a good visit with my grandparents. When my dad wasn't in prison, my mom didn't know that my dad would show up at all hours of the day or night and take me away from my grandparents. My grandparents always told me never to say anything to my mom or she would not bring me to see them anymore. If the cops picked up my dad and me, they would take me to my grandparents' home, and we would not speak of it again. The police never questioned the situation. They knew who my dad was, and they knew where he lived. Dropping me off at my grandparents' was good enough for them. In their eyes, was I as low as my dad? Was I in the same category as he was? The shame of my dark secret affected my inner self-worth, my self-esteem. Although my heart told me I wasn't worthless and I knew God loved me, I couldn't shake off the effects these situations had on me.

My grandparents bought me a little black-and-white television and put it in the bedroom. Every Saturday night, I would lie in bed, eat junk food, and watch my favorite television program, *The Love Boat*. One night, my dad showed up really late and told me to get ready because I was going with him. I had no idea where we were going. I could tell he was already mad, so I didn't ask any other questions. As my grandparents watched in silence, I didn't want to make eye contact with them for fear they would begin to argue with my dad and end up hurt. I put my sweater on, and I followed him out of the house. He took me to the neighborhood bar down the street from my grandparents' house, Art's Bar.

I walked through the old-fashioned Western swinging doors. The musty smell, the thick cigarette smoke in the air, and my inability to see clearly gave me a feeling that not only was I not allowed in there, but also that this place was trouble.

The bar owner said, "It's illegal for her to be sitting at the bar with you, Robert."

My dad ignored him. They were terribly afraid of him, and I was so embarrassed to be with him. I knew I was not supposed to be at a bar establishment, much less sitting at the bar. So to cool the waters, I asked my dad for a nickel so I could play some music on the jukebox. I played the song "Angel Baby." I played it repeatedly. Another man was sitting at the bar with us.

He asked, "She's been playing that song over and over. Can she play another song?"

That set my dad into a mad rage. I never understood how he could become so angry in a split second. *Is this the rage that comes from going to war?*

"Don't be mad. I'll pick another song," I said.

But it was too late. My dad got up from the bar and began arguing with this man.

"Stop!" I screamed as I tugged on his arm.

I begged him, but he already had that look in his eyes, and I knew it was too late. He was at that point of no return. I was crying. I was so nervous that I was shaking uncontrollably. They pushed through the wooden swinging doors and began to physically fight on the sidewalk in front of the bar. The man had no idea who he was messing with. My dad had fought in the Vietnam War. He knew how to kill! He was on drugs and alcohol. In his rage, he became the devil himself. I was so terrified. Both backed away from each other. They were in that wrestler's stance with both arms out to the side. They were circling each other. I noticed that my dad had a fork in his hand. I freaked out! I was screaming and crying out for my dad to stop, but it was too late. He went toward the man and pushed the fork into the man's body. He stabbed him. He turned to me. His eyes were huge. He looked possessed. Or was it lucifer in life form?

He told me, "Run down the street and turn right at the gas station. Run all the way up that street, and grandpa will be waiting there for you."

So I took off running. I was crying hysterically and I couldn't breathe. I was at the point of passing out. I knew I had to rise above the situation I was in and mentally overpower what had just happened and convince myself that it was all going to be okay. I kept running and finally got to the gas station. At that point, I recognized where I was. I can still recall the brightness of the gas station lights. I felt as if they were turned on extra bright to spot me and uncover what just happened. I made a right and ran. I ran past my mom's old house where she had lived when she met my dad. I ran past the house where my grandma and I would stop and take a break from carrying the groceries. I ran past the apartments where my dad lived with Elaine. When I reached my friend's home with the Christian mom, I knew I was two houses away. I finally reached my grandparents' house.

My grandpa was not outside, like my dad told me he would be. The gate was already locked for the night, so I had to jump it. I then ran down the driveway and up the stairs. I began to frantically bang on the door. Because my grandmother was hard of hearing and my grandpa slept like a log, I had to pound for what seemed like an hour. My grandpa finally came to the door. I was cold, freaked out, and crying. I told them what had happened. As always, I knew the police were going to show up and lay us all down on the floor with our legs spread as they searched the house for him. We waited and waited, but they never came. My dad was eventually caught and arrested. I never found out what the charges were, but he spent a long time in jail. We never spoke of the incident again. Ever!

I always felt as if I walked around with a secret. I didn't want anyone to know because they might not want me around. They might not want to be friends with me. The only people who knew about the type of dad I had were my grandparents' neighbors and my family (to a certain extent). His time in jail would fluctuate. At times, he was locked up for months. Other times, it was a couple of years. It seemed like it was never long enough. When my dad was in jail, the neighborhood was happier. The neighborhood kids would play jump rope, hide and seek, and hopscotch. People would hang out in their front yards, chatting comfortably. I was at peace when he was locked up. In my little mind, I was in control of my life when he was in jail. But when he was released, an inner fear, a heavy weight, was placed on me. I walked around scared, even when I wasn't with him. When word got out that my dad was out of jail, everyone on the block stayed inside. There were no kids; no laughter. As the years progressed, we became outcasts. The kids on the block were not allowed to play with me. I would knock on doors and ask to play with my friends. I would hear their moms tell them no. I later would see the same kids playing in their yards, behind their fences. The only neighbor who did let me play with her kids was this Christian lady, Lecha. She never seemed to be afraid of my dad. She is actually the one who first invited me to her church, the Salvation Army.

I felt like such a bad person. I felt embarrassed to be seen, so I played inside the house a lot. I wanted to scream out that I was a good person and that I wasn't a part of the things my dad did. For years I walked around with this secret part of me. with this secret part of me. But after my dad died, I felt as if I had to divulge my past to anyone to whom I got close. For some reason, I felt I had a moral obligation to tell people who they were getting involved with. It was as if I had done something wrong.

In my heart, I knew I wasn't a bad person. When I would step into my other life, my normal life, I felt strong and somewhat in control. My mom was the only stability I knew in life because she would somehow always make things okay. I knew she was in control of our home life and I could concentrate on being a kid. The Lord blessed me with wisdom at a young age so I knew a better life was out there. I thank the Lord for giving me the strength to trust Him with my life.

At the age of eleven, I began my relationship with God through His son Jesus. The church I attended always reassured me that I had a Father in heaven who is all-knowing and perfect and loves me more than anything. Knowing that, I convinced myself that I was going to leave a much better legacy than the legacy and turmoil my dad had left me. I wanted to prove that. I wanted to prove to the world that I wasn't the same as my father. I now think about the mistakes I made in my life, and I feel that I made the worst mistakes and made the worst choices when I surrounded myself with people who were not goal oriented. They were in the same category as losers. I don't know why I thought it was okay to be around those people. My mom worked so hard to show me the good life, teach me how to choose quality friends, and work hard to have nice things. When I was going down the wrong road, I would always pray and ask God to help me, guide me, and never leave me. He answered my prayers.

In everything, I strive for the best. I don't let obstacles get in my way. I seek to have better things in life. I make every effort to have a long-lasting marriage. I strive to raise my kids with high morals and standards. All these years, as I've worked my way to success, not only was it for my kids, but deep inside I wanted people to see that I was not a failure. I wanted to send a message that I took a chance and put my faith in God. And it worked! He saved me! I'm fine. I made it, and so can you!

About eight years ago, I made a new friend. She was so much fun, and she loved to eat good food and go antique shopping, just like me. We really connected. She was down-to-earth, and she came from the same area where my grandparents lived. As we grew closer, I began to spend more time with her, and I felt as if I needed to tell her about my past. I felt so obligated that it would bother me every time I saw her. One day, I got up the courage. I called her and told her. Of course, she was sympathetic, as everyone is when I tell them about my dad and my past. But it felt different that time. It felt weird.

Why did you tell her? It's none of her business.

That was eight years ago. We are still friends, and she never brings it up, but she was the last person I ever told. Well, until now. I am telling my story because now I know and I am 100 percent positive that I am not ashamed or humiliated any longer. My dad's actions (or anyone else's actions) do not reflect badly on me or taint me. I was a child, and I was not responsible for my dad's choices. Now I choose to share my story so other war daughters and all who have had trauma in their lives can know this truth sooner and never be humiliated. My wish is that you do not waste precious years living in shame. We've had enough to last a lifetime.

My desire for you is that you to let go now. Today! Don't waste your time being affected by bad choices other people have made. If you are suffering with insecurities, shame, embarrassment, emotional issues, or any other crippling effect, I hope you can clearly see that you are not at fault. You are only at fault for not changing it. After reading this book, if you still choose to live in the same manner or don't seek help or follow your dreams, then that is your choice. Enough is enough. No more blaming and feeling sorry for yourself! I have told you that, by faith in God, His salvation, His mercy and grace, you have the power to change your future! I am walking, breathing, and living proof that it can be done! One hundred percent positive!

What I Know

When you first laid your eyes on me,

I was told you fell in love with me.

I was the angel in your life.

You loved me.

My innocence took your heart.

The need I had for you must have taken you by surprise.

You must have loved me,

but you chose wrong. Now you're gone.

Nothing can be fixed,

but I know you must have loved me.

I Never Felt Love Like the Love They Gave Me

My grandparents adored me. Grandma was a short, little thing. She had long, grey hair, which she always wore it in a bun. She had a dark complexion, and she never wore makeup. She was the best cook in the world. She spoke broken English, but she could sure tell you off in English if you crossed her. Grandpa was a passive, short, fat man who loved to collect junk. He was always whistling. When Grandma would feed him too much, he would grow out of his pants. Instead of buying new pants, he would loosen his belt and use a safety pin to hold the pants together. He would gain and lose, so he never wanted to buy more clothes. When they would bicker about unimportant issues, my grandma would stick her tongue out at him the moment he turned his head. I thought that was the funniest thing ever. Grandma always got up early to make his breakfast and pack him a lunch before he left home for work. She was a good wife, and she took good care of him. They were so cute together. They loved each other.

Every Saturday, Grandpa would walk to the local fruit stand and buy me oranges, cherries, mangos, and anything else I wanted. I was the apple of their eyes, and they were the apples of my eyes. They loved me very much, and I knew it. I never doubted that. I had a gap in my heart, and I yearned for my dad's love, and my grandparents filled that gap. They had a look in their eyes that cried out immense love for me. They would hug me, kiss me, buy me anything I wanted, and cook homemade meals for me. They depended on me. They needed me. I was the only good thing in their lives.

I have the best memories of my grandparents' house. It was warm and colorful. It always smelled like good home cooking. I had many toys in the big house next door, which they were using for storage. Their house was love to me. It was where I received the most love growing up. It was also where I saw the most pain. It's where I witnessed living hell.

They had the best of intentions. They never wanted me to know about my dad's addiction and his lifestyle. They wanted me to see the man they wished he were, but they couldn't stand up against him. To do so would only land one of them in the hospital because my dad was physically abusive to them. So when he would take me from their home, they were helpless. Each time my dad was in jail, we would visit him wherever he was being held. My family would take my grandparents and me to visit him, no matter how far the prison was. Aunt Dee, Uncle Gary, and Cousin Dina would pick us up in their brand new two-toned blue Ford, and we would drive to whichever state institution my dad was in. They would make it an event. The ride was the best. We would pack fried chicken, soda, chips, and all kinds of junk food for the ride. They would play Fats Domino, Glenn Miller, and Elvis on the way there, and we would all sing along. I had never heard that type of music before, and I learned to love it. That music still brings back good memories of my aunt and uncle. In my young, inexperienced head, I was always able to see the better side of things. I knew life was good. I could smell it in the air.

My grandparents and I were most at peace when my dad was in jail. It was the best time and from when I have the best memories of my grandparents. We were able to live a normal life and have a stress-free, normal relationship. The other me, the fearful child, did not interfere. She was locked away too. I could be happy, vibrant, and full of life. I could be myself. I would play with the kids on the block all summer. I would come in to eat and go back outside to play. I would climb the fruit trees, pick the fruit, and eat it while sitting on a branch. My grandpa would holler at me to get down, but I wouldn't listen. My grandma had many antiques. When I was tired of playing outside, I would come in the house and go through all of her antique jewelry. She would get so mad when I would take all the jewelry out of her boxes, but I knew I could get away with anything. They were so good to me. They were gold. They never said a harsh word to me. They never called me a name, and they never laid a hand on me.

As I got older and went into junior high school, I had to lessen my visits to them. My dad was too dangerous to be around, and I was no longer oblivious to the fact that I could really get hurt around him. I was tired of him and his lifestyle. My grandpa would call me every week and ask if I was coming over that weekend. He would offer to take me shopping. He would tell me he went to the fruit stand and had all my fruit waiting for me. He would ask why I wasn't coming over anymore. I would lie and tell him I was really busy with school and work. It hurt me so much to do that to them. I could hear the disappointment in his voice as he would hang up the phone. It killed me every single time, but I had to immediately block out the feelings. I was at an age when my body was developing. I was no longer a child. I was a young lady. My imagination ran wild. I feared I could be raped at places where my dad would take me late at night. Or I could be sold into prostitution. After all, some of my dad's girlfriends were questionable in that area. I had to protect myself. I had to disconnect at all cost, even if that meant giving up my grandparents, my biggest love at the time.

But I went to visit them one weekend, and my grandma had her arm in a cast. She had taken a fall from the top of the stairs and tumbled all the way down to the bottom. It was a miracle she didn't die. I should have suspected something wasn't right with the story, but I didn't. Shortly after her fall down the stairs, I received a phone call at home that my grandmother was in the hospital. It was the summer before I started high school. When I walked into her hospital room, I could see that she was no longer coherent. Her hazel eyes were open, and she was staring at the ceiling. I waved my hand over her eyes to to let her know I was there. She tried to moan something, but soon after, she was gasping for air. I had gotten there just in time. Less than fifteen minutes after I arrived, she took her last breath. As I pulled the blanket over her face, I silently told her it was over now. She was free to rest from the hell she had been through. And I was free of the worry I had for her. I couldn't cry. I was so hardened by then. I looked at my grandpa sitting in a chair at the foot of her bed. He had no emotion. He just stared at her body. He didn't say a word. He had such an empty look in his eyes, as if he had departed his body. To this day, I have never seen that look in another human being. I found out later that my dad had pushed my grandmother down the stairs because she hadn't given him money for heroin. He was the reason she had her arm in a cast. I also found out that he was abusing my grandfather, beating him up and taking all his money for heroin.

My grandmother died on June 25. Almost a year later, we got a call at home. My mom hung up the phone and called a friend and asked her to go with her to my grandpa's house. As she sped out the door, she said, "Don't answer the door for anyone. Pretend you're not home."

I was home alone that day, so naturally, I was afraid. I didn't know what was going on.

Why couldn't she tell me?

My mom had never told me to not answer the door to anyone. I was the eldest of the three girls. I knew better than to answer the door to a stranger. When she said that, I knew something was really wrong. A few hours passed, and all was calm. I was sitting on the couch, watching television. Suddenly, I heard what sounded like someone hollering in our townhouse complex. I turned off the television and got down on the floor by the window. I slowly picked up a small piece of the corner of our curtain to peek out of the window. It was my dad! He was shouting my name loudly. My mom never told him exactly where we lived, but he had an idea. People there didn't really know what my dad was like. Thankfully, they never had the opportunity to experience an episode. I was so embarrassed. My two worlds had never collided before. My friends, the boy I liked who lived across from us, and the neighbors could see and hear everything that was going on. I had never allowed my dad to cross into my life at home. He had no place in it, and now he was here in real life! I wanted to vomit. I was so scared. I didn't let him know I was home, but now I knew that something really bad had happened. But I didn't know how bad it really was going to be. My mom came home later that night. When I heard the keys jingle, I ran to the door, wanting to know what was going on.

"Who called you earlier?" I asked.

My mom answered, "After your grandmother died, I gave our phone number to the tenant who rented the downstairs apartment. I told him to call if anything ever happened to your grandpa."

As she hugged me, she told me, "Your grandpa had a heart attack and died."

"My dad came looking for me." I said.

But she minimized the situation and blew it off as my dad being crazy. My poor mom knew the truth, but she couldn't bear to tell me. I couldn't get any more information from her. My grandpa had had a heart attack. That was all she said.

I didn't go to my grandpa's funeral. I couldn't handle seeing everyone. I couldn't bear their sympathetic gestures. So I went to the mortuary before anyone else arrived and said good-bye to him. As with my grandmother's death, I still couldn't cry. I was just glad it was over. My grandparents were my only real connection to my father, and now I was free. Both of my beautiful grandparents were now resting on the other side. And my dad was nothing to me. I didn't feel as if I had to preoccupy myself with his well-being.

I let a couple of months pass after my grandpa's death

before I felt like I was able to address the will. His loss really affected my emotional stability. I was still holding on to untold secrets and unaddressed pain. But I wanted to get it all over with, so I borrowed my mom's car. I drove to my grandparents' home, where my dad was now living. It felt strange to walk down that long driveway where I once had played. I felt empty. When I got to the top of the stairs, I had a really awful feeling that I shouldn't be there alone with my dad, but I went inside anyway.

My dad was sitting in a chair in the living room. He looked horrible. His hair was overgrown. He had raggedy clothes on, and he looked really depressed and lost. I knew my dad must have been lonely living there without my grandparents, but he seemed odd that day. Something was different about him. We were alone, and we were talking one-to-one, adult to adult, stranger to stranger, but with nothing to hide. We were discussing our next steps with the will and the estate. The will I had in my hands named me as the executor of the estate. I was to decide how I was going to handle the liquid assets, the free and clear property, the antiques, and everything else that was fully paid for. But, to my surprise, my dad also had a will and it wasn't the same one I had. I guess he couldn't tolerate the guilt any longer. He began to cry and recount how my grandpa had died. My dad said he and my grandpa were arguing because my dad wanted money, but my grandpa wouldn't give him any, so he pushed my grandpa, and my grandpa fell to the floor. He then sat on top of him and began to choke him. My grandfather went into cardiac arrest and died. He said he got so scared that he shoved my grandfather's body under the bed to hide it. But before he did that, he took my grandpa's pants off to get to his wallet. Then he shoved the body under the bed and left to look for me.

As my dad recalled the events, he cried like a baby. He kept telling me how sorry he was. He was bent over in his chair, almost in a fetal position. I was standing up, looking down on him. I could see the dandruff in his hair, and I could tell he had not showered in days. I wanted to get out of there. I sure as hell wasn't going to comfort him. I let him cry, and I showed no feeling. I couldn't! As he recounted my grandpa's death, second by second, I died. The pain I was feeling was so severe. It hurt me to my core, to the absolute bottom of my stomach. I wanted to kill him. In the bottom drawer of the dresser chest, my grandma had kept an antique gun that was always kept loaded. It was an arm's length away from me. She used to tell me that if anyone ever broke in the house or if I was ever in harm's way, I should get the gun and protect myself. I wanted to get the gun and shoot him! I wanted him to die! He had hurt the two people I had loved the most. He had taken away the most special people in my life at that time, the people who showed me the most love and made me aware that I could love back. He had taken them from me.

I held my vomit. He repulsed me. I didn't kill him because I knew he wasn't worth it. He was the lowest of the low, and I wasn't going to ruin the beautiful life the Lord was making for me. I just stood there in shock and stared at him with a blank face. When he saw I had no emotion and that I wasn't going to love him through this, like I used to when I was a little girl, he regained his composure and sat back up. He wiped his tears and stood up tall as if to show pride. I looked at him straight in the eyes.

"You're going to have to live with this the rest of your life. You'd better ask God to forgive you,"

I had to leave. I got in my car as fast as I could. I was crying uncontrollably, and I could barely drive. I was inconsolable. I had no one to comfort me. I was hurt, and I was angry.

Why didn't anyone tell me the truth about the day my grandpa died?

I'm sure it wasn't a secret. If the neighbor had called my mom, then that tells me people knew. They forgot to tell me? Was I in a house with a murderer? My grandparents were gone from this life, and I was left alone with him. No one would ever understand what my dad had put me through. I knew I was going to suffer alone in silence. I had to figure out how I was going to get over what I had just learned and not let it weaken me. To think about what my grandparents went through was too painful, so I kept it inside and never told a soul what I knew. Whether they knew or not, I was not going to talk about it.

Everyone thought I didn't know, and that is how it was left for years. In order to overcome the pain and keep myself from feeling guilty that I hadn't saved my grandpa from my dad, I had to tell myself that they had created my father. They had chosen to bring this little baby home and raise him. I hadn't created this situation. I was born into it. I was helpless, and I couldn't help them even if I wanted to. I was too young. This period of my life was too painful. I cannot allow myself to think about the inner pain my grandparents had felt. I could not bear to think about what my grandmother had gone through when her little boy, the son she cooked for, nurtured, and gave her life to, pushed her down the stairs. Her pain must have been so deep. How did she sleep? After my grandmother died, I can't imagine the fright my grandfather must have felt, being there in that house by himself and knowing that, any day, his son could snap and really hurt him. You see, I loved my grandparents so much that all this is too difficult and too painful for me to digest, so I must leave it in God's hands.

For the record, my grandpa's body didn't have any bruising or evidence of trauma, and my grandpa did have a history of heart disease.

The death certificate reads myocardial infarction, or heart attack.

Therefore, as God's chosen people,

holy and dearly loved,

clothe yourselves with compassion, kindness, humility,

gentleness, and patience.

Bear with each other and

forgive whatever grievances you may have

against one another.

Forgive

as the Lord forgave you.

Colossians 3:12–13

This Wasn't the Love I Was Looking For

From the time I was six years old, I was always in church on Sundays. I would usually go with my grandma, but, when I wasn't with her, I would wake up at six o'clock in the morning and walk to church by myself. It was always very important to me to go to church. When I moved to the townhouse complex, I was at an age where I was becoming interested in boys. I wish I would have paid attention to the sermons at church or maybe have had a mentor who would have helped guide me through this time of my life with Godly guidance. I wish someone would have told me to never take my eyes off the Lord. If someone had, I wish I would have listened. I would look outside and see the kids in the townhouse complex still playing late at night. They had so much freedom. I felt I was missing out because I was cooped up inside. Sometimes doing fun things and hanging out with the popular crowd leads to trouble in the end. I am a perfect example of that.

It was the summer of 1981. We had just moved to these beautiful townhouses on the hill, in one of the best areas of our city. Coming from the ghetto, these were the most beautiful homes I had ever seen. The night my mom took us to see our new home, I couldn't believe it. As we drove up the hill, there was building after building and huge parking garages under each building. The bright lights in the garages fascinated me. Every garage was well-lit and bright with beautiful expensive cars of all sorts. The complex had huge trees all over. The grass was well-kept and green. It had a huge pool area with a separate Jacuzzi and a covered BBQ area. We never had a pool before.

"Is it really true? Are we really going to live in these beautiful new homes?" I asked my mom.

Most of the people who lived there were young working professionals with nice imported cars and plump wallets and young families with children. It sure was a fun place to live back then. I was so naïve and truly innocent. I wasn't one of those kids who would disobey their parents. I was never sassy with my mother, much less my father.

I went from having tons of friends to having zero friends. I was so bored at my new home. On a very hot summer day, I saw kids at the pool laughing and playing. Even though I was shy and they were all new to me, I was willing to make new friends. After all, this was my new life. I soon managed to make many friends there. We would all play together, girls with boys, and we all got along. We had so much fun.

This boy lived across from me in the next building. From my balcony, I could see into his house and vice versa. He was so cute. I was immediately caught up in his hazel eyes. I had never liked a boy so much. Deep inside, I knew he was off-limits because I didn't know anything about him. In my thinking, I wasn't as well off as his family and he was out of my league.

I knew I had to get to know him a little more. Did he go to church? Did he love the Lord?

What if he's into doing bad things?

These items were important to me.

I never heard him talk about God. But he was so much fun. With the self-esteem issues I had and all my insecurities, I never thought he would want anything to do with me. I thought he was too good for me. I wasn't pretty enough, plus he really didn't speak to me.

One day, a bunch of kids in the neighborhood decided to walk down the hill to the liquor store to buy water balloons and have a water balloon fight. I didn't have a lot of money, so I was only able to buy one pack. All of us kids were spread out all over the complex. We were hiding behind buildings and bushes and bombing each other as we ran. I went back to the bush where I was hiding my balloons and realized I was out. I saw "hazel eyes" running toward me. As he was ready to slam me with a balloon, I put my hand up in the air to stop him.

I screamed, "Wait! I'm out of balloons!"

As my arm went up, our hands met in the air. His hand clutched mine. We both froze for a moment as we looked into each other's eyes. He had the most beautiful hazel eyes I had ever seen. That was it! I knew he liked me. He just didn't want to say anything. Or could it be I was just imagining the magnitude of that moment? He didn't know about the other part of me. He had lived here all his life. His family had money, and we didn't. I wasn't from that part of town. I was holding a secret.

After that moment, while I was still looking for more words, he said, "I'll cover for you, and we'll be a team."

As the other kids noticed I was out of balloons, he would yell out, "We're a team!"

Wow! It was something so small, but, to me, it had a huge impact on my heart. I had never experienced such a nice boy who was willing to take care of me and look like a fool to his friends for taking a girl's side. I never had a boyfriend. I really wasn't allowed to, but I was going to now. I didn't want him to like anyone else. He had to be mine.

My new best friend and I began to hang out exclusively. Anytime we kids would hang out, I would stand by him. We would share candy, soda, or whatever. It was a true partnership. We clicked. Little by little, I began drifting away from my foundation. I stopped going to church. I didn't want him to know that I was so in love with the Lord. I didn't want him to think I was a good Christian girl. The practice of attending church and finding peace and comfort in God's love is what got me through the years of pain with my dad, my mom's divorces, my loneliness, and my own inner pain. Now I was going to voluntarily give it up for love on earth, love I could actually touch in real life. I wanted him to think I was cool. I thought that if he knew I was a churchgoing girl, he would not like me.

We dated for three years. The early years were so fun. They were heaven on earth. We were inseparable. His parents were divorced, and his mom was a workaholic and never home, so we spent every minute we could together. He was my best friend. We would take walks together, do homework, listen to music, and hang out with our friends. And in the summer, we spent our time swimming in the pool and being normal kids having fun.

The latter years were a living hell. I had volunteered

myself for a bad relationship and walked away from the Lord and what was pleasing to Him. He turned out to be a monster. He began using drugs, and he became another person. I can't count the beatings, the black eyes, and the bruises. He emotionally, verbally, and physically abused me. He was my dad all over again, but he was worse in my eyes because I was the one getting beat this time around. My dad had never laid a hand on me.

I couldn't tell anyone. I was so disappointed in myself. I was so ashamed and embarrassed that I had allowed myself to be so weak and vulnerable. I would make up lies about the bruises. I would tell my mom that I had walked into a tree while playing or that my friends and I had been roughing each other up. I was so broken. The worst part is that I knew better. The Bible says to not be unequally yoked. I chose him. I wanted him. Now I didn't know how to get rid of him. He was the devil in real-life form. I was in such a bad place. I lost my smile. I lost my direction and positive outlook on life. I felt so hopeless.

One day, as I sat on our sofa and casually talked on the phone to my friend, my mom was sitting next to me and noticed a bruise on my arm. It was so large I couldn't hide it, especially with the short-sleeved blouse I had chosen to wear that day. She lifted up my sleeve and immediately knew.

"Is he hitting you?" she screamed.

I began to cry. I didn't answer her, but it didn't matter. She bolted out the front door and ran over to his house. She was banging on his door. Before his mom could get the door fully open, my mom busted into their home, found him standing in the hall, and beat the crap out of him.

His mom stood by and watched. When my mom finally calmed down, his mom said that he had deserved it.

A few weeks later, he walked up to me when we were at school. We walked the long way to one of my classes. As we approached the back of the building where my classroom was located, he began to pull my hair and call me names. Soon after, I was able to get to the phone booth. I called my mom and told her what he did. I didn't expect her to come to my school, find him in the crowd, and beat the crap out of him again in front of everyone. My poor mom, what must she have felt to see her daughter go through the very same things she had suffered through? If I had been her, I would have wanted to die. I finally broke all contact with him, and he went on to the next girl.

I can't stress enough how important it is for a little girl to have that father figure in her life. The role a father plays in a young girl's life is what helps mold her self-image and self-worth. If a dad is telling his daughter that she is his princess, his joy, and his life, she is less prone to seek the attention of a boy who hurts her, a bad boy.

It is so powerful when the dad is a strong leader in the home, the anchor. If a divorce is inevitable, the best thing a dad can do is keep an extremely close relationship with his daughter and take the role of the man in her life. It's hard for some men to know how to adapt to this role because they themselves never had a good father figure. But that is no excuse. A dad should spend a lot of one-on-one time with his daughter, ask her questions about what is going on in her life, participate in activities she likes, and know who her friends are and let them be a part of the visits.

Moms should also practice these traits with their children. I tell you this truly very private story because all of you mothers, daughters, and single women need to know that when you have a home in which the father is absent, your girls and your children feel it. Be aware and proactive. Talk to them. Keep them close to you emotionally. You will have to be mother and father at times. Take your role.

I want you to know there is hope! Don't give up on the Lord! John5:11–15 tells of the time when Jesus healed the crippled man and told him to take up his bed and walk. I am living proof of healing. I was freed from the pain and hurt. I have picked up my bed, and I am walking. It does get better.

Once you are awakened to the knowledge of the power that God can have in your life, you are awakened to the fact that you can live a good life with a strong, vibrant spirit excited to wake up each and every day. Sadness becomes a foreign feeling. You never forget, and you can sometimes cry about your past. But, all in all, you are free from that life of feeling trampled over, smashed down, left out, and passed by.

So, what are you waiting for? ***Get up and walk!***

Make level paths

for your feet

and

take only ways

that are

firm.

Proverbs 4:26

Lucky Girls

A fifteen-year-old girl who has Victoria Secret underwear? I thought that was the coolest thing ever. I went over to my friend Lisa's house after school to study. Lisa wanted to get out of her school clothes, so we went upstairs to her room so she could change. As she undressed, I noticed her undergarments. They were so cute. The bra and underwear matched. They had lace all over. I was so envious. I wished I could have nice things too. Her home was a large two-story in the nicest neighborhood. The entire house was so clean. I could tell that her mom took care of making that house a home. I could feel it. It felt right. It felt like a Brady Bunch home. I wanted her life. I began asking her personal questions about her home life, but then I quickly stopped my inquiries. Lord knows I didn't want her to ask me about my home life because I would have elaborated and divulged too much. But I wanted to know so much more. I wanted to see a picture of her dad. I wanted to know if he was good to her.

Was he nice? Did she feel loved by him? Was she his princess, daddy's little girl, like I had seen so many times on television?

Coming from a broken home where money was

scarce, being raised by a single mom whom I hardly ever saw, having a father addicted to heroin, and longing for normality, seeing Lisa's life made me feel worse. I felt so low, so unworthy of her friendship.

I thank God because He made me see that I would one day create the type of life I wanted for myself. Since that day, I've learned that whenever you encounter a situation where someone has more than you have, be happy for that person. Thank God that person is not struggling. Why would you want that for another human being? Instead, remember who provides the blessings in the first place. I was fortunate enough to be blessed with God's wisdom, and I knew that one day I was going to be able to buy myself nice things.

Don't allow yourself to feel sorry for your situation. Turn these feelings around. Make them a catapult for you to strive to be the best you can be. Strive to be better than what you have been taught. Finally, don't dwell on what others have. Be happy for them! Just know, without a doubt, that your Father in heaven knows everything you desire, and leave it at that. That must be good enough for you! It must!

Keep your lives free

from the love of money

and be content with what you have

because God said,

"Never will I leave you;

never will I forsake you."

Hebrew 13:5

More Than Anything, I
Love You More

Everyone wants to be loved. Humans have a natural desire for unconditional love. We want someone who will stand by our side, even at our lowest points in life. We want someone who will give us unconditional love and support, even if we make life-changing mistakes. We all have a need for a life partner who will never lose that sparkle in their eyes when they look at us. We want someone who will make us feel special every day. This desire begins at birth. And there are millions of people who will live their entire lives searching for this love, and they will never find it. They will never know it, never experience it, and never have that peace in their hearts. My desire is to give people hope and reassurance that it is possible to have unconditional love.

When I was in an abusive situation, I felt so helpless. I didn't have anyone to turn to. I didn't have my dad to protect me from this animal who was punching me in the face. Do you know how terrible it feels to think you are all alone in this world? To know that, if something bad happens to you, you'd better know how to get yourself out of it? Although I had my mom, she had my two little sisters to worry about. I had to learn how to take care of myself.

I had to learn that I was alone and no one was going to rescue me from anything. No one was there to catch my fall. That is why I held on tightly to the fact that Jesus was my only savior. He would never leave me or turn his back on me, and he could make my dreams come true. Hearing that He loved me so much and that He died for me, I had to believe. I had to give it a shot.

Since I was a little girl, I always knew about God, Jesus, and the Holy Spirit, but it was a religious thing to me. I couldn't see Him, so how could I trust Him? I would pray to Him and hope He would answer my prayers, but it wasn't until I was eleven years old that I really decided to give in. My little friend Mina, who lived across the street from me, invited me to Victory Outreach Church. We sat next to her mom in an auditorium. I loved the worship music immediately. That morning, the pastor, Sonny, told the congregation to make multiple prayer circles all over the auditorium. That was so weird to me, but I got into a circle and held Mina's mom's hand. As the people in the circle began to take turns praying, each one was praying for the same things I silently prayed about. They prayed for help, loved ones, and forgiveness. I never heard people cry out to God in that fashion. Their words were so filled with emotion. As they prayed, they cried. A powerful feeling overwhelmed me. It was too big for me to handle. I tried to keep my composure, but I couldn't. I completely lost it. How embarrassing! I wasn't crying. I was sobbing uncontrollably. My nose was running, and I was a mess! Mina's mom put her arms around me. "Why are you crying?" she asked.

"I don't know." I answered.

"Do you want Jesus to come into your heart?" she softly whispered.

All I could do was nod my head up and down. I said the prayer of salvation:

Jesus, I know you died for my sins, and I believe you are the son of God. I want to surrender and put my trust in you. Please enter my heart, and live in me as my savior.

I had to take that chance and let Him in. I was at the end of my rope. I knew I was not going to be able to handle everything my dad was putting me through. I knew I was hurting, and that I was beginning to be bitter. I knew I had a whole life ahead of me, and I was trying to hang onto the lighter side of life. He was my only hope. Pastor Sonny would preach that we had a Father in heaven and He was our true Father. In my young eleven-year-old head and in my little heart, I had to learn how to replace my earthly father with my heavenly Father. I had to learn how to make God the Father into my protector, my security, and my rescuer. I still couldn't see Him, but now I knew for sure that He was there. I could feel Him now.

I hope and pray that as I have spilled my heart out to you, you will not let it go in vain. The countless hours I spent crying as I typed and revisited horrible memories were so you could have proof that there is hope. It's time for you to be honest with yourself and decide if you are ready to take a chance on God. Decide right now that you are done with the past. Decide right now that you will no longer put your dream life on hold. Decide right now that you are taking control of your future. Decide right now, not tomorrow and not after the next chapter, that you are going to do what I did. You are going to give God a chance.

Let love be your greatest aim;

nevertheless, ask also

for the special abilities

the Holy Spirit gives, and

especially the gift of prophecy,

being able to preach

the messages of

God.

1 Corinthians 14:1

I Was Ripped Off

After my grandpa died, my dad continued to live in my grandparents' house, in the upper-level apartment. The downstairs unit still had a tenant. The house on the side was still full of the junk we all stored there over the years. After my grandpa died, I found out that the will I had was voided out by another one that my grandpa and dad had drawn up. It named my dad as the executor of the estate and completely removed me. My dad told me that he forced my grandpa to change his will. Because I had no power over the estate, my dad's attorney would not talk to me or meet with me without my dad present. I left it alone. I figured I would have to wait until my dad had passed before I could get the estate back. I now know that I could have contested the will, but I was too young back then. My dad had taken advantage of me.

One day, I got a call from the tenant living in the downstairs unit. She told me that I had to get there quickly because there had been a fire. My grandparents' house, the entire building, had burned to the ground. Everything was gone. She said she had not seen my dad for days. I got in my car and drove over there. Not knowing what to expect and not wanting to see my dad, I drove by very slowly. I couldn't believe it. It was true. It had vanished. It was all over. Even if my dad died and I became the executor of the estate, it was all gone. I would be executor of the dirt. The one and only thing my grandparents left me was gone. My college money, my financial security, and my jump start in life—gone! It was a very somber moment, yet I had no emotion. I think I was in shock. I couldn't find the strength to stop the car, so I kept driving.

A few months passed. I made contact with my dad again. He told me he had sold the land and we needed to meet with the attorney to finalize the proceeds and divide it between us. I told my dad I would help him buy a small little home so he could live in it. The day we had to meet with the attorney to settle the estate business, I went looking for my dad in the streets because he no longer had a home. I knew I could find him somewhere in the neighborhood. As I drove down the alley behind the grocery store where my grandma and I used to shop, I found him. I saw someone sleeping in the bushes. I called out his name. Without even recognizing me, he got into my car. He smelled so badly, like urine and booze. I was so embarrassed to take him to the attorney's office. The attorney basically told me to wait outside his office while he spoke to my dad. So that's what I did. They let me into his office once they had settled business. I was in the dark. I had no choice but to follow my dad's lead and hope he would be generous with me.

Later that year, my dad cleaned up his act. He had an apartment, and he was talking about buying a little truck and starting a carpet-cleaning business. He had reunited with Larie. But he seemed weird with me. He became very arrogant. He was no longer talkative with me. My presence seemed to threaten him. I had a strange feeling that he considered me an outsider. It seemed as if he were hiding something. All I know is that the property was fully paid for, free and clear of debt, and that my dad was supposed to give me half of the profits.

A few months passed and I received a telephone call. My dad was on the other line. He wanted me to meet him at the bank. I didn't know what to expect. I didn't want to get my hopes up about finally getting my inheritance. I arrived at the bank. We walked over to the teller booth. He withdrew $1,000 and turned to me. In front of the bank teller he said, "Don't ever say I never gave you anything."

He put the money in my hands.

As we walked out, he told me, "Call me in one week, and we'll go to the cemetery where your grandparents are buried. We'll buy two headstones for their graves."

"I'll call you," I said.

I didn't.

And we know

that all that happens to us

is working for our good

if

we love God

and are fitting into

His plans.

Romans 8:28

I Couldn't Believe My Eyes

Have you ever driven by a bus stop in the city and seen a homeless wino either sitting on the bus bench or sleeping on it? Have you ever seen a wino bum so drunk that he is talking to and laughing to himself? I have. Did you know that many of those people are our veterans? I have always been interested in knowing their life stories and how they ended up on the streets. How about the people who beg for money at the freeway off-ramps? How did they get to that point in life? And where do they go at night? Do they have families? Could they be victims of war?

I was working in downtown Los Angeles in a beautiful building, ARCO Towers, on the thirty-third floor. Our office took up the whole floor, and we had a full view of the city. It was so beautiful, especially at night. When possible, I would stay late just to stare at the city lights in the dark. My life was so different from what it had been. I had changed a lot, and I had come a long way from my beginnings. I had a good job. I was working with well-educated people, and I was learning so much from them. I wasn't just learning about the business finance world, I was also learning about that good life that I could smell in the air when I was little. It really did exist. It was out there, and I was going to have it. I was promoted to the mortgage banking department. There, I learned about stocks, Wall Street in general, business finance, and the inner workings of the real estate and mortgage industries. I thank my bosses; I must have driven them crazy with all my mistakes, I was so inexperienced and naïve to the real world, but I was truly enjoying myself and learning so much. Life was great!

It was 5:00 PM, and I was done for the day. It was a beautiful afternoon so I decided to take the local streets home instead of the freeway. Taking the streets was the long way home. It meant I would have to drive down Whittier Boulevard, a huge main street that ran from downtown Los Angeles, across many neighborhoods, and ended in the suburbs. There are traffic signals and many people along this route, but I was in the mood to drive. Along with many traffic signals, there are many bus stop benches. I reached a stoplight. As I was waiting for the light to turn green, I was looking around at the happenings. As I looked to my left, I saw this man on a city bus bench, completely drunk. He had no front teeth, and he was bouncing up and down on the bench, laughing to himself. He looked a little familiar, but no, he couldn't be.

As I looked a little closer, it was my dad! I had not seen him for a couple of years after my grandpa died. I was shocked to now see him in this situation. He had sunken so low. I wanted to keep staring, but the light turned green, and I had to keep driving. What was odd is that instead of feeling sad, I felt no connection. He was from another lifetime. He was a stranger. I felt so liberated. It was done! The Lord had completely taken away the hurt my dad had inflicted on me and replaced it with a heart of strength and courage. No longer was I weak to the past. I had moved on. I felt sorry for the guy, but he had chosen his journey on this earth. I hadn't. As I stepped on the gas pedal, I turned up the music and continued on my way home. It was the last time I saw my war dad, my veteran.

War dad, war daughter, war mom, people, there is hope, and there is healing. All you have to do is believe!

When you are praying

first forgive

anyone you are holding a grudge against,

so that your

Father in heaven

will forgive

you

of your sins too.

Mark 11:25

What Happened to My Dad

By 1989, I was married, and I had a beautiful little boy. I felt a need to have my dad see his first grandchild, so I planned a day where I would drive into the city and go look for him. On that day, I gave my precious little boy a nice bath. I put baby powder all over him, and I dressed him in his best outfit. We got in the car and drove to the old neighborhood. I don't know what I was thinking. My dad didn't have an address, but I figured I would run into him. I drove up and down every street I thought he'd be. I drove around for hours, but I couldn't find him. So I drove back home and figured I would have to look for him another day.

By this time, I had purchased my second home, and I was still working in downtown Los Angeles. My new home was really far from work, so I would take the Metrolink train every morning at 4:50 AM. There was this cute, petite lady with reddish-blonde hair that she curled at the ends. She had the most gorgeous, big, brown eyes, and she would sit across from me every day. I sat with the same group of people every day, and I would always comment to my friends that this particular lady would always stare at me. I could be in a conversation with my friends, and her energy was so strong that I could feel her looking at me. Every time I turned to look at her, our eyes would meet. We would lock for a few seconds, and I would turn away because I didn't understand what was happening. She seemed harmless.

One morning on the ride into LA, I decided to confront her because I was tired of feeling weird. That morning, I purposely sat next to her. I must have made her feel uncomfortable because I always sat with my group of friends.

I finally got the nerve. "Do you know me?"

"I don't. I just love your eyes."

Isn't that funny? I thought she had beautiful eyes too. Needless to say, I befriended her, and we became Metrolink buddies.

One morning, I asked, "Where do you work?"

"I work for the Los Angeles County coroner's office in the records department."

My heart fell. I felt as if a heavy ball had hit me in my stomach. It was all so clear now. She was supposed to get my attention. From what I understand, if there is an unidentified dead body, it is taken to the coroner's office. There is a department where all the records of each body are kept. It contains detailed information, including the autopsy reports, sketches, and physical descriptions.

"Can you look up someone for me?"

I didn't divulge my relationship to this person.

"Give me the name and any other information you have. I'll look it up."

Being that I didn't know my dad's whereabouts, all I had was his name to give her.

As I got off the train, I put it out of my mind. I went

on to the office, as I did every morning. I didn't think she would find him although I went back and forth between believing he was dead and believing he would live a long time. I waited all morning. It was almost lunchtime. I had not received a phone call from her, so I figured she couldn't find a file with his name on it. Then, right before I was to leave for lunch, my phone rang. It was her. She had found him. I wanted the file faxed to me right away.

I pleaded, "Fax it to my office!"

But she was reluctant. "I'll come to your house tonight and drop off the file."

I refused. "Is it really him?" I was insistent.

The other side of the line got quiet. She softly asked, "Juju, is this your dad?"

"Yes. But I'm ready to see it. I can handle it."

"Are you sure? Are you sure?"

After convincing her, she faxed the report. Because it was around lunchtime, a lot of people were out of the office, including my boss. I had the privacy to review the report. I ran over to the fax machine and nervously waited for it to ring.

I thought I was ready for what was to come, but I was wrong. As the fax sheets were coming through, I was trying to read every line. It all didn't make very much sense to me, and I kept telling myself it was the wrong person. Then a drawing of the corpse began to come through. I could see the sketch of this person lying on the street. As the drawing of the body reached his arm area, there was my confirmation. The tattoo on his right arm said "*Juju.*" He had gotten that when I was a little girl. It was my dad. I had to keep my composure. I was at work. I wanted to cry, but I didn't. I didn't know if I was sad or happy. I felt relieved. He was gone. I never had to look over my back again. There was nothing and nobody to be afraid of now. I was free.

The police report stated that a business owner had called about a dead body in the alley behind his store. They found the body by a large, black, city trash dumpster amid trash and debris. He had been dead for three days. The flies were nesting in his nose and eyes. The body was decomposing quickly from being in the sun for three days. The report stated that his right hand was still wrapped around a bottle of wine and there were numerous bottles of Thunderbird wine around him. According to the coroner's report, he died of liver failure. No recent drug use was evident. And they labeled him Robert, a known local transient.

Behold, I stand at the door and knock.

If anyone hears my voice and opens the door,

I will fellowship with him

and he with me.

To him who overcomes this world,

I will let sit beside me on my throne,

as I also overcame

and sat down with my father on his throne.

He who has an ear, let him hear what the spirit says.

Revelation 3:20–22

Epilogue: Ode to the Soldier

Being the daughter of a war dad, I accept the fact that all this horror my dad created could have transpired because of what he saw and experienced in Vietnam. It was too much for him to cope with, and he lost it. That's why I don't hang on to the pain of his mistakes. To do so could lead to judging him. He screwed up, but I'm fine, so I forgive and move on. I am fully aware that I couldn't possibly begin to comprehend the terror, fear, and pain soldiers must have felt fighting that guerrilla war. I have respect and gratitude for my dad's role as a soldier. A special place in my heart is grateful to this man, my father, who sacrificed his life not only for me, but for you and our country. I came to a greater understanding of this on Memorial Day in 1991. I was sitting with my baby and watching a Memorial Day celebration on television. A feeling came over me. I actually felt as if I had a personal connection to Memorial Day. I don't know if it was because I was now a parent and a functioning member of society that I had a better understanding of the sacrifices a soldier makes for his or her country. I felt as if I, a citizen of the United States of America, should pay my respects to all these men and women who died fighting for my baby boy and me. And although my dad didn't die in Vietnam, he slowly died after the war.

Because I hadn't known that my dad had passed, I obviously hadn't attended his funeral. I later found out that he had been given a military funeral service. The only attendees were Larie and a few others. I wish I could have been there when the guards shot off the twenty-one gun salute. I wish I could have formally closed that chapter in my life and his. No matter what happened in the past, I wish I could have sent him off to the other side. I found out where he was buried. A few weeks later, I went to the cemetery. As I walked over to his grave, I read the other headstones, and I wondered what their stories were.

Did they create hell on earth for their children too?

When I found his grave, I couldn't cry externally, but my soul was sad. My heart cried. I bent down to put flowers on his grave. I had no words. As I turned to walk away, I quietly thanked him for his service to my country.

I have not been back since.

Greater love has no man

than this,

that he lay down his life for his friends.

John 15:13